Straight-Ahead Jazz Drumming

A Guide to Developing a Driving, Swinging Beat

Plus! Variations, Embellishments, Exciting Tension-and-Release Techniques, and More

by Jeff Jerolamon

Edited by Rick Mattingly

ISBN: 978-1-61774-274-3

HAL•LEONARD®
CORPORATION

7777 W. BLUEMOUND RD. P.O. BOX 13819 MILWAUKEE, WI 53213

In Australia Contact:
Hal Leonard Australia Pty. Ltd.
4 Lentara Court
Cheltenham, Victoria, 3192 Australia
Email: ausadmin@halleonard.com

Visit Hal Leonard Online at
www.halleonard.com

To the memories of Jamey Heath, Brian Trainor,
and Jerry Allen Jerolamon

Contents

Audio recorded at **SP Estudios**.

Recording engineer: **Sergio Peiró**

Preface

It's somewhere in the mid 1970s, about 1:00 A.M.; I'm at a coffee shop on Sheridan Square in Greenwich Village with my best friend and musical colleague for almost 40 years, drummer extraordinaire Rick Fiori. Coffee, tea, and blueberry muffins are on the table as well as several napkins with musical notation scribbled on them. We've just gotten back from the Village Vanguard where we could have been listening to anybody from Elvin Jones with his band, Eddie Gladden with Dexter Gordon, Victor Lewis with Woody Shaw, Tony Williams with Hank Jones, Bill Goodwin with Phil Woods, Jack DeJohnette with his band, or any other outstanding band of that time. And there we were again, at the same coffee shop trying to digest and decipher what we had just been listening to… a scene that would repeat itself many more times to come. As long as New York City was offering, we were willing to accept.

That was over 30 years ago, and the hunger for improvement is still going strong. Nowadays there's so much to draw from, CDs, DVDs, the Internet—all wonderful material ripe for the picking. Yet, one can't spend his entire life taking without giving something back. Just as sons and daughters are destined to become the next generation's mothers and fathers, music students are tomorrow's performers and/or teachers.

As a performer, I've been lucky enough to have had the opportunity to travel to many parts of the world. And now, with the publication of this material, hopefully the knowledge I've accumulated over the years will also reach students all over the globe. I hope they enjoy working on this material as much as I did putting it together.

Jeff Jerolamon plays exclusively NP drums, Murat Diril cymbals, Remo drumheads, Morgan Mallet drumsticks, and Viana Artisan snare drums.

Acknowledgements

I would like to thank:

my parents and brothers for putting up with all the "noise"; my daughters Julia and Ana May for existing; Johanna Spanjerberg who supported me in this project from the beginning; Carmen Nikol for her many years of support; Maria Jose Costa for her support and generosity; and most of all, Rick Fiori for his inspiration, enthusiasm, colaboration, friendship, and unconditional support.

Introduction

 Track 1
(an introduction)

A "language" study for drummers on how to accompany a soloist in a "straight ahead" jazz context.

Roy Haynes, Max Roach, Philly Joe Jones, Elvin Jones, Tony Williams, Art Blakey, Kenny Clarke, Jack DeJohnette, Jimmy Cobb, Louis Hayes, Arthur Taylor, Billy Hart, Charlie Persip, Albert "Tootie" Heath, Danny Richmond—man, just saying those names out loud makes my fingers snap, my toes tap! I can hear the band roaring as these great drummers shape, inspire, and swing the soloists to play beyond their limits. They are the forefathers of modern jazz drumming, our teachers, and our musical role models. And although some of these drum giants may be stylistically opposed, they all seem to be united by a common musical "language," and their masterful control of this "language" gives them all the ability to:

1. swing like crazy;

2. make a soloist sound even more exciting than he actually is;

3. enrich the music by adding detailed rhythmic counterpoint;

4. do all of the above in a highly personal manner.

So what's stopping you? There's no mystery here; you have all these great examples to draw from. Just listen to them, assimilate them, and you've got it! Well, if you can do that, you don't need this book.

However, if you are listening to CDs and you can't seem to put your finger on what's happening; or you think you hear it, but when you listen back to your own playing, it's not quite right; or you've collected lots of nice "licks," but you don't know how, when, or where to play them; or you're simply just not satisfied with your playing, then this study should be of value to you.

Notation Key

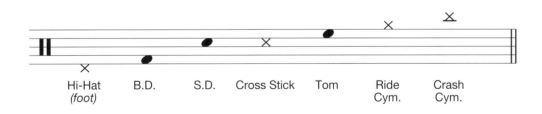

THE JAZZ LANGUAGE

All musical styles have their own language, and jazz is no exception. A musical language gives musicians the means to express themselves with their fellow bandmates in such a way that everybody understands each other in whatever style of music they may be playing. Here, we will take the straight-ahead jazz idiom and approach it the same way as you would in learning a spoken language. We'll break it down to its basic vocabulary, learn to use each new "vocabulary" word in sentences, and then learn to be expressive with it. With time, we'll also see how we can put more drama into our playing. Just as literature and film do this through problems and solutions, we achieve this effect in music through tension and release.

Though references will be made to certain key players (particularly in the listening part of our study), in these pages, you'll find no transcriptions or analysis of any of our drum heroes (John Riley already has several great books out on that), or attempts to influence the student to play like any specific drummer. My feeling is that if you learn the "language," you can then go on to find your own way of expressing yourself, thus converting this study into a musical launching pad for finding your own voice, whatever that may end up being.

MUSICAL DEVELOPMENT

Through time, you may discover that the drummers you like best aren't the ones who put the most drums in the music, but the ones who put the most music in the drums. Let's face it, it's not just about *what* you play; many times what makes a certain figure so exciting is *how* it's played, *when* it's played, or *where* it's played. We all have the same basic vocabulary to choose from, so one of the main differences you hear from player to player is a matter of what someone chooses to play at a particular time. The good players make the right choices. This is due to musicianship, not to drum technique! In order to learn how to make the right choices you must:

1. Learn the vocabulary and and be expressive in the language.

2. Spend many hours listening to the masters.

3. Play with other musicians as much as you can.

As far as learning the vocabulary and being expressive with it is concerned, you can get off to a great start by practicing the material in this book (you're never done; music is endless).

Listening to the masters is just as important as practicing! For a guide to what you should be listening for, refer to the Listening Guide at the back of the book. There you will find a list of drummers to listen to who have mastered the jazz language. It will also explain to you how to listen for the concepts and techniques discussed in this study.

As soon as possible, you've got to get out there and play. Never turn down the opportunity to play with musicians who have more experience than you. The ideal situation is when you're the worst musician in the band. That's when you learn the most!

THE DRUMMER'S FUNCTION

It's very important that you know what your responsibilities as a drummer are in a straight-ahead jazz context.

To look at your function within the band, you must look at the relationship the drums have with the other instruments in the ensemble. Assuming that the band is made up of a rhythm section of piano (or guitar), bass, and drums along with a soloist, traditionally, this is how it works:

The bass outlines the fundamental harmony notes with a walking quarter-note pulse. The drummer supports the walking bass line with a strong "4" feel on the ride cymbal, almost inaudible quarter notes on the bass drum (feathering), and the hi-hat played on beats 2 and 4.

The pianist's function is to feed the soloist the chord changes, and to be sensitive to any chord substitutions the soloist may be implying with his note choice. At the same time, he (or she) creates a rhythmic dialogue with the drummer's left hand and bass drum accents.

Lastly, the soloist looks to the rhythm section to be supportive with all of the above, while being sensitive to the dynamic and intensity level of the solo. Rhythmic interplay may also occur between the soloist and rhythm section.

SINGING THE TUNE

Singing the tune is an essential discipline in this study. It's our musical mantra that allows us always to know where we are in the structure, freeing us from worrying about counting measures. It also obligates us to always put our "drumming" in a musical context.

I remember the first time I heard about the concept of singing the tune while playing. I had gone to the Village Vanguard with my drum companion and friend Rick Fiori to hear Elvin Jones. As always, Elvin played magnificently that night. I was particularly dumb-founded as it was the first time I heard him play live. After the gig, Elvin and his wife needed a ride home. Rick, who was a friend of the family (unbeknownst to me), offered to take them. As we rode home, Elvin explained to us that everything he plays comes from the tune, and that he always sings the melody in his head while he's playing. That was in 1974; we've put it in practice ever since.

You don't have to sing well. I'm the world's worst singer (and I defy anybody to differ), but that hasn't stopped me. Besides, no one's going to hear you anyway. You don't have to know the words (if there are any), you don't have to sing perfectly in tune, but you do have to sing in tempo and in meter. As a start, you'll need at least one blues and one 32-bar tune with either an AABA form or ABAB. If you don't know what I'm talking about, I suggest that you find a more experienced musician to explain song structures to you. It's absolutely essential for this study.

All exercises, whether written or improvised, are to be practiced with the discipline of being accompanied by singing a tune. To begin with, try to find easy tunes to sing, without a lot of notes and that sound good at different tempos.

TUNE LISTING

Throughout the study we'll be referring to the jazz standards listed below. You should be familiar enough with them to be able to at least hum them so that you can play the exercises and follow the tracks on the CD in context.

Autumn Leaves	All of Me
There Is No Greater Love	Take the "A" Train
I Love You	Tune Up
Softly as in a Morning Sunrise	How High the Moon
Just Friends	I Got Rhythm
Bye Bye Blackbird	Lullaby of Birdland
There Will Never Be Another You	But Not for Me
What Is This Thing Called Love?	

THE RIDE CYMBAL

The first thing you hear with any jazz drummer is the ride cymbal. It's his stamp, his trademark, and the most predominant part of his playing. This is why the first word to be learned in our new "language" is the traditional ride cymbal rhythm. There are many subtle differences from drummer to drummer in their ride cymbal sound, which make this topic appear to be a very tough one to tackle. However, when you strip it all down to its "basic bones," there are certain traits that all the great drummers have or had. Once these traits are mastered, you can go on to phrase the cymbal in a more elaborate way (if that's the way you hear it), knowing with confidence that it's going to be driving and swinging!

The first is **a clear quarter-note pulse**. The cymbal beat should imitate a walking bass feel. This is logical since the walking bass and the ride cymbal drive the band. The marriage of the two should be a happy one, and the best way to prepare for that is to have your future "spouse" in mind during your training. So it's not only essential that you know what a good, swinging walking bass should sound like, you should be able to sing one as well. Don't worry about the pitches, just get the right feel. Be able to sing that feel as you play the ride cymbal.

Secondly, the cymbal rhythm should **flow in phrases**, and not sound like it's playing from beat to beat. We accomplish this by learning to sing a tune as we play the ride cymbal rhythm. This will make the rhythm flow more as it automatically puts things into a context.

Evenness is also essential. Whatever your sound is on the ride cymbal, make it an even, uniform one. The evenness gives it that repetitive dance quality and sets up a "home base"—that is, a place to come back to—when you start creating tensions with your accents.

Playing the Ride Cymbal

The evolution of the ride cymbal in jazz history is a study in itself. Swing drummers and some of the early bebop drummers got sort of a floating, happy, tap-dance sound while driving the music with a strong 4 on the bass drum. This was done by playing the cymbal as a three-note pattern, starting on the second and fourth beats, that sounded like "(lang) splang a lang, splang a lang, splang a lang," etc.

However, as bebop came to the forefront, innovators like Kenny Clarke and Max Roach taught drummers to lighten up on the bass drum. Over time the bass drum was played softer and softer until it was played so lightly they referred to it as "feathering." Without the prominence of the bass drum, the cymbal now had a greater responsibility to drive the band. Its tap dance-like quality gave way to a more driving 4 feel. With all the subtle nuances you can hear from drummer to drummer in their cymbal beats, even to this day, all the greats seem to have this clear, driving quarter-note sound.

As a starting point, to go for this sound, try to hear the cymbal beat with the following perspective: starting with a pickup, "gadang dang gadang dang gadang dang" etc.

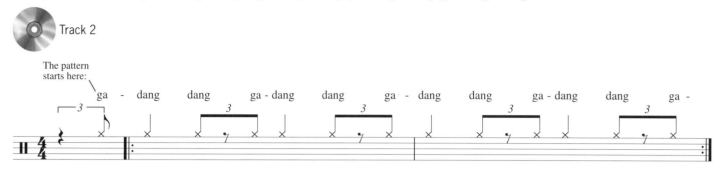

Make sure that you have two separate strokes (a double followed by a single) that outline the quarter-note pulse. You want to emulate a walking bass feel.

Try to hear the cymbal pattern in two parts, first as "gadang" then "dang." The "dang" part is easy, but the "gadang" needs some special attention. The trick is to have the first note (ga) drive into the second (dang). Don't try to accent or make any special effort, just let the stick bounce naturally. To work on this, try the exercise below.

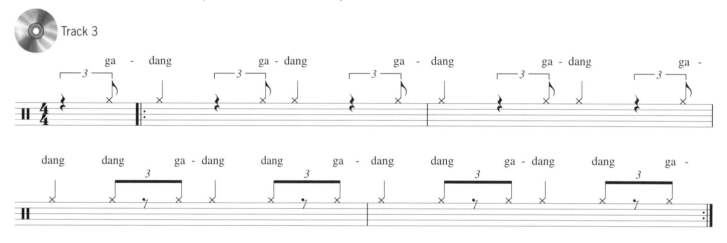

Make sure that in the third and fourth bars, the quarter notes are even. Think of a walking bass and imitate the feel.

Up until a certain tempo, the subdivision for the traditional jazz cymbal pattern is in triplets (unless you want to imply a double-time feel).

Track 4

However, once it reaches a certain velocity, the triplet subdivision starts to bend towards the eighth note. To know at what velocity you should start bending the triplet subdivision, try this simple rule of thumb: when the tempo is so fast you can't sing triplets any more (diddily diddily diddily diddily), start to stretch it. But even though you may not be playing strict triplets any more, the triplet subdivision should still be implied. We do this by making sure that there's a space between the "gadang" and the "dang." Try to stay with that space and the quarter-note feel for as fast as you can before resorting to the inevitable single three-note motion.

Track 5

As you start to get the right feel for the cymbal, add the hi-hat on beats "2" and "4," and then the bass drum on all four beats played as softly as possible. This bass drum "feathering" technique is more difficult than you may think and doesn't sound good if it's not under control, so be careful about bringing it on the gig.

 Track 6

Once you're able to get a nice "walking bass" feel on your ride cymbal, make it flow more: sing a tune at the same time as you play the cymbal, imagining that there's a walking bass. Don't worry about counting or which bar you're in, just let the song guide you. Sing different tunes with different structures at different tempos.

Playing the Ride Cymbal Consistently

When playing the ride cymbal, also keep in mind that **consistency** is very important. Once you have your ride sounding the way you like it with a nice, clear, flowing, even sound, you want to make sure that it stays that way, no matter what you may be playing with the other three limbs.

Control of your stick height is very important. If your stick height remains consistent, so should your sound. Keep in mind that the volume and clarity of your ride sound will also be greatly affected by how far the stick is coming off the cymbal.

If you're looking for a big, forceful cymbal sound, then you will be coming off that cymbal as far as you can get away with, without being too loud for the band. If that's the case, I recommend a dry sounding cymbal, to control the overtones.

However, if you're looking for a more floating type of ride sound, then you've got to develop a light, dancing, bounce technique on the cymbal. In this case, you should choose a nice, dark, wet cymbal that will do the work for you.

Keep in mind also that, the louder you play the ride, the more it will gobble up the subtleties of the rest of your kit. Always be aware that you're your own acoustic sound technician; you control the balance between the different parts of the drumset.

With practice, you'll also discover that you can play the ride cymbal effortlessly, free of tension, with no sense of weight whatsoever. Every tempo has a certain maximum stick height in which you can maintain this sensation.

EMBELLISHING THE TRADITIONAL RIDE CYMBAL BEAT

Once you get a nice "walking four" feel on your ride cymbal, it's time to start embellishing it with "comping" figures—that is, hits with the snare drum or bass drum that will either rhythmically coincide with the cymbal rhythm or will fill in the spaces.

We'll be approaching these "comping" figures as we would the vocabulary of a new language. Each figure presented, once learned, should be practiced as we did the cymbal rhythm—that is, always while singing a tune. As the vocabulary increases, you'll have the responsibility not only to include the new figure, but also the previously learned figures in your improvisations. Pick tunes with different structures and tempos, don't count, and let the song be your guide.

All figures will only be two beats long, and even though they may be written in eighth notes, phrase them as discussed in the ride cymbal study.

The first figure (Figure 1) of our vocabulary is just the cymbal rhythm. This figure will put space in your playing so it breathes. Figure 2 is the next word of our "vocabulary." Once you're able to play it comfortably, it's time to apply it. To do this, play choruses on a tune, just like you did with the cymbal (Figure 1), only this time, sometimes include Figure 2.

To give you an idea, here's an example of what you could do over a blues.

Track 7
(over a blues)

*A bass drum hit on the "1" of your entrance is always appreciated by the band.

As you can see, I'm interchanging the two figures as I hear it. Now you try it.

Notice how Figure 3 doesn't rhythmically coincide with the ride cymbal, but rather fills in the hole of the missing eighth note, thus affecting the general rhythm between all of the limbs.

Below you have a chorus of the blues, not only utilizing Figure 3, but also including Figures 1 and 2.

Track 8

Play your own improvisation using Figures 1, 2, and 3 over a blues and other song structures as well. Vary the tempos.

Check out the following variations on Figure 3.

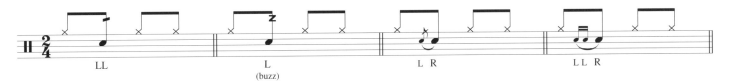

These variations can be applied to any future figures presented that include an eighth note with the left hand that doesn't rhythmically coincide with the ride cymbal.

Try playing choruses with some of these variations.

Track 9
(one chorus of "Bye Bye Blackbird" utilizing Figures 1, 2, and some of the variations on Figure 3)

With the remaining figures of our "bebop vocabulary," follow the same process of improvising choruses over different tunes and tempos. Always include the previously learned figures as well as the new one. As your vocabulary increases, experiment with combining different figures or limiting yourself to certain determined figures.

Track 10
(one chorus of "Just Friends" exclusively utilizing Figures 1–23)

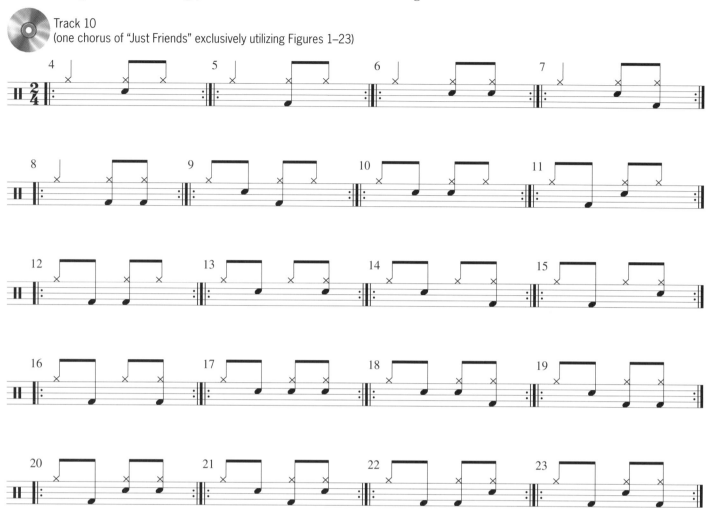

Triplet figures will only work up until certain tempos. Once the tempo is so fast that they're uncomfortable to play, don't play them!

(Although written in triplets, the cymbal remains constant.)

Track 11
(one chorus of "Autumn Leaves" exclusively utilizing Figures 1–60)

To give your improvisation more shape, try playing the bass drum on the "1" of the first bar of a new section, e.g., the bridge or second half of the tune (not all tunes have a bridge) and the top of the chorus.

Then, to give it even more shape, play a figure at the end of a section that leads into the "1" of the next section. See example on the next page.

In order to see how this works, let's take a tune with an AABA 32-bar structure. In the first bar, I give a bass drum hit on the first beat. I proceed to play figures from the learned bebop vocabulary as I hear it throughout the chorus. However, two bars before the bridge at "B" (it doesn't have to be two bars; it could have been one bar, half a bar, or whatever), I pick more intense figures that lead up to the "1" of the bridge. I then continue mixing the bebop vocabulary until, once again, right before I arrive at the chorus, I play something from our repertoire that gives a little tension before resolving it on the "1" at the top of the chorus.

Track 12
(over "All of Me")

Now try playing choruses on an AABA-structure tune. Apply your bebop "comping" figures. Choose figures that lead into the "1" of the bridge and the "top" of the tune as in the above example.

Track 13
(one chorus of "I Love You")

TENSION AND RELEASE

Music (a definition): *"Music is a continuity in time of a sequence of greater and lesser tensions conveyed through the medium of sound and creating an aesthetic sensation."* William A. Humenay, *Music Composition Book V*

On the previous page, you had an introduction to how tension and release works. As you will discover, a great way to put drama and excitement in the music is to create tension and then resolve it. The greater the tension, the more emotion you will evoke when you release it. When done tastefully, this powerful tool can make soloists sound more exciting than they actually are!

Throughout this book we'll be studying different techniques and figures to create tension and also where and how to resolve it. As we're doing this, we must always keep in mind that this is not an individual effort, but a team effort. It's the rhythm section creating the tension, not just the drummer, and if the bass player is walking, then it really comes down to the communication between the piano player and the drummer. Don't forget, just as you have to be grooving with the bass player, the piano player's also busy listening to any harmonic variations the soloist is implying. So all of this is easier said than done!

When creating tension, it's often best to work backwards from its release. That is, if you know where you're going to resolve it, then you can judge how long you want that tension to be, and where to start it. Traditionally, tensions are resolved on the "1" of the first bar of any given section of a tune. The reason for this is that the harmony also resolves there, so you have the harmonic and rhythmic tension resolving at the same time.

A tension figure may be suggested by the drummer or the pianist. In either case, the other player has the option to play a similar figure, a contrasting figure that sounds good with it, or leave space and maybe just make the resolution hit.

The degree of the tension is determined by:

1. how much it rhythmically goes against the grain of the 4/4 flow;

2. the length that it's played (the amount of beats or bars);

3. the volume at which it's played.

Tension and release will be an ongoing theme throughout the rest of this study. Take it seriously, listen to the CDs, hear how the masters create tension and resolve it, and arrive at your own conclusions!

Let's investigate in more detail how, with the learned vocabulary, we can create tension to be later released with a "1" on the bass drum, marking the entrance to a new section of the tune.

One of the most common and effective techniques to create tension is to play a repetitive figure several times before resolving it. Below are some figures from the bebop vocabulary that work well. They're divided into rhythmic types.

Type 1

Type 2

Type 3

Type 4

Here's how we can apply some of these figures in a repetitive manner to create tension. In this first example, we are creating two-bar tensions that lead into the "1" of each eight-bar section of the chosen 32-bar tune. In the first bar of each section, I've written out some of the more common figures that come right after a resolution on "1."

Track 14
(over "How High the Moon")

Here it is with three-bar tensions. Keep in mind that this is an exercise; in an actual playing situation, you wouldn't be mechanically playing a set number of bars of tension in every section of the tune. In fact, you might not be setting up tensions at all in some of the sections. Or maybe you'll just create tensions before the bridge and the top. It all depends on what the situation calls for!

Tensions can be of any length. In this example, they are all four bars long. With the following exercise, as with the previous ones, be sure not to count bars, but to use the song that you have chosen to guide you.

Now play choruses of any tune, applying tensions of different lengths. Mark different parts of the tune, and always keep in mind the more important ones like the top and bridge (or the second half of the tune). In the 12-bar blues, apart from the top, the "1" of the fifth bar (where the harmony goes to the IV chord) should also be considered.

Track 15
(one chorus of "What Is This Thing Called Love?")

Track 16
(several choruses of a blues)

Here are some triplet figures from the bebop vocabulary used as tension figures. Notice how, in the following 32-bar chorus, you have tensions of various lengths. The longer tensions are saved for the entrances to the bridge and the top.

Track 17
(over "Take the 'A' Train")

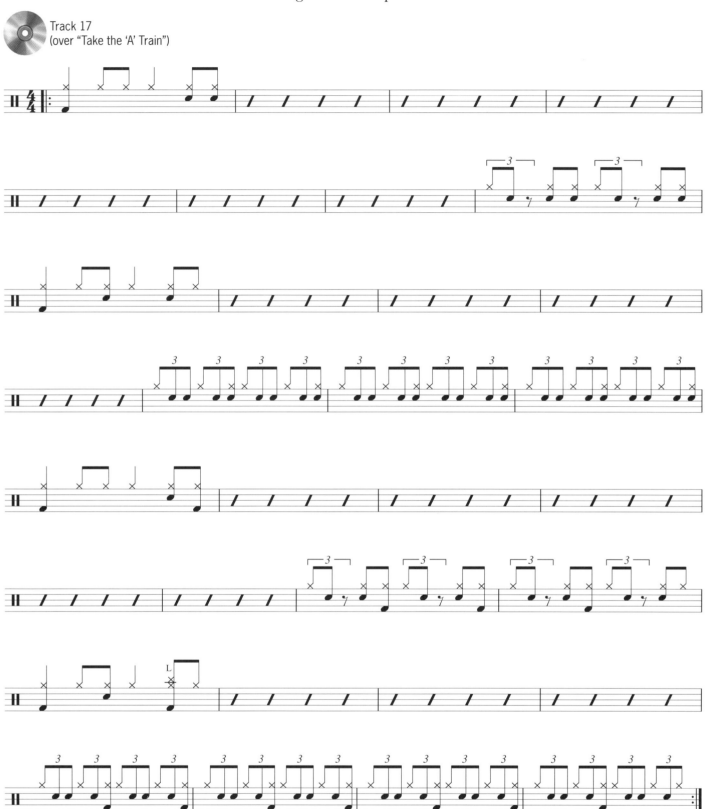

Play choruses of a tune utilizing these triplet figures as tensions. Vary the lengths of the tensions, and choose tunes with varied structures and tempos.

Sometimes, in the last bar of a section, a fill is played leading into the "1" of the next bar (the first bar of the next section), very often marked by the bass drum and a crash cymbal. The fill can serve as a brief tension figure in itself, or as a preparation to the resolution (the "1") of a longer tension.

The general idea is something like this:

Any sticking will do, and don't confine yourself to just the snare drum; add the toms as well.

You could start the fill anywhere in the measure.

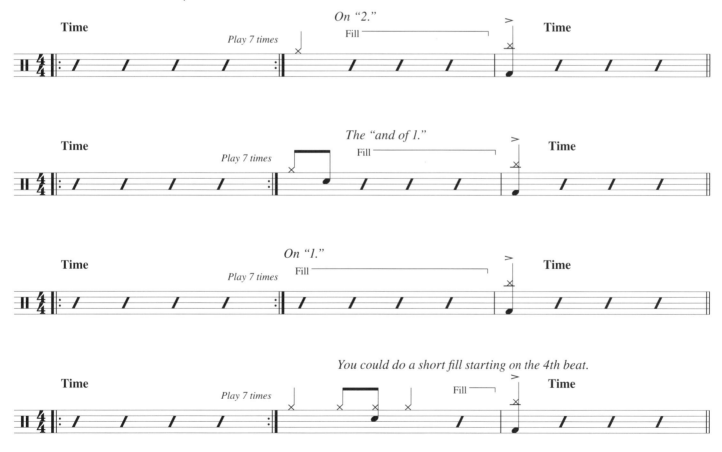

It all depends on the effect you're after.

Play several choruses of a 32-bar AABA tune. Play a fill leading up to the bridge and to the top, sometimes as the end of a tension, sometimes alone.

 Track 18
(one chorus of "Softy as in a Morning Sunrise")

RIDE CYMBAL VARIATIONS

When the 1960s rolled around, straight-ahead jazz drumming began to take on new innovations. As the music began to open up more, so did the drumming. Elvin Jones, followed by Roy Haynes and Tony Williams, began to bring exciting new innovations to the table that would change drumming forever.

One of these changes was in the ride cymbal—not only how it was played, but also in the way it was approached. Up until this time, the ride cymbal drove the band, while the left hand and bass drum were used for accents to give interest and create tension. With this new concept, the cymbal alone would swing the band, be constantly varying, and at the same time contribute to the setting up of tensions to create excitement in the band!

In the next few pages, we're going to isolate the ride cymbal and approach ride cymbal variations just as we did with the previous comping figures. We'll break it down to just four simple patterns over two beats. Once they are mastered, it's just a matter of combining them in the way that you hear it, while, of course, singing the tune of your choice.

Although at first glance there appear to be many ride cymbal variations, we can break it down to a vocabulary of just four basic rhythms over two beats:

By mixing these four different rhythms you can come up with lots of nice combinations. But first, play each one repeatedly, say four times each, going from one to the next without stopping. Make sure that you maintain the same "walking bass" feel as you go from one figure to the next. As you do this, you should discover that each one of these patterns has an individual character of its own.

 Track 19   Pattern 1 is, of course, the traditional ride cymbal rhythm and is the most driving of them all.

 Track 20   Pattern 2 has just the opposite effect. When repeated, it pulls the music back instead of driving it forward. In a real playing situation, avoid excess repetition of this figure.

 Track 21   Pattern 3 is simply quarter notes. When used repetitively, it can be quite effective. When mixed with the other figures, it has a sort of neutral effect on the flow, creating the feeling that you're waiting for something to happen.

 Track 22   Pattern 4 is the shuffle rhythm, which also has a driving sound.

Now let's see how we can combine these four two-beat patterns.

One way to conceptualize cymbal variations is to use the traditional cymbal rhythm as a point of reference to start and come back to. Notice how the example below begins with various repetitions of the traditional pattern before starting to intertwine the other three patterns. Also notice how, from time to time, it reverts back to the traditional pattern. You don't have to approach it like this, but I think it's a good way to start out. Sing a 12-bar tune while playing the example below. Make sure that you maintain a "walking bass" feel.

Track 23

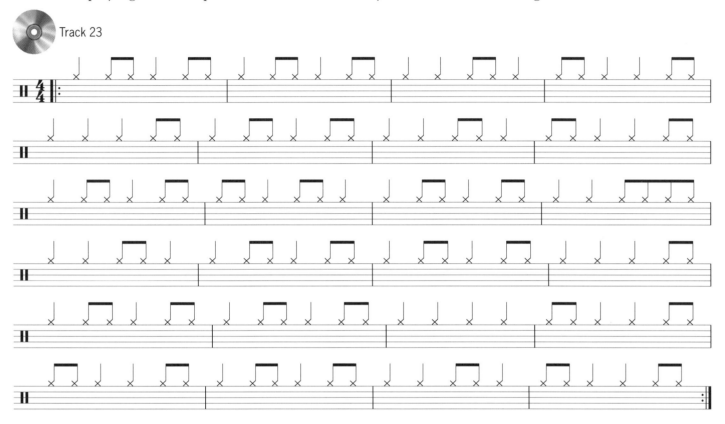

Now try the following exercise. You have two bars written; improvise a cymbal rhythm for the two-bar answers. Keep singing the 12-bar blues!

Track 24

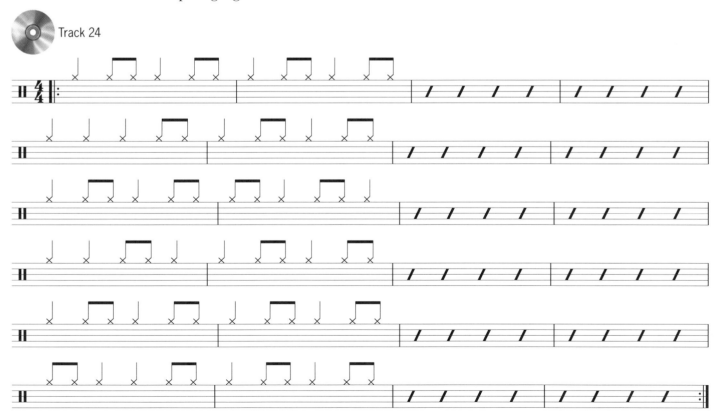

This time you have four bars written; you answer with the next four.

 Track 25

It's time to do it on your own. Play several choruses of the blues while varying the cymbal pattern. Then do the same on other song structures. Be sure to change up the tempos.

 Track 26
(one chorus of "Just Friends")

EMBELLISHING RIDE CYMBAL VARIATIONS

Now that you have your cymbal variations sounding good alone, it's time to "dress them up" with the rest of the drumset. When embellishing cymbal variations, we'll use two basic approaches: "rhythmic unison," in which everything you play with your left hand, bass drum, or hi-hat hits at the same time as the ride cymbal, and "linear," where nothing you play with the other three limbs rhythmically corresponds with the ride cymbal.

"Rhythmic unison" is a more condensed, solid sound, while the "linear" approach is a broader, fuller sound. The most usual is a combination of both, with the "linear" becoming the favored approach in slow to medium tempos, and "rhythmic unison" dominating in faster tempos.

Let's take a look at the "rhythmic unison" approach first. When adding the left hand, bass drum, or hi-hat (which may or may not be played on "2" and "4"), we simply make sure that they fall at the same time as our improvised cymbal rhythm. A hit anywhere in the bar can sound good; just make sure you don't come down on beats "1" or "3" too much.

In order to get the idea, work your way into it by playing these four-bar phrases four times each. Then construct eight-bar sections by playing one of the written four-bar phrases followed by four bars of your own. Finally, improvise an entire chorus on your own.

Track 27
(one improvised chorus over "There Will Never Be Another You")

24

Don't just limit the written hits to the snare drum; move them to the toms and also play some of the hits on the bass drum and the hi-hat. Play the previous exercise again, this time substituting the hits on different parts of the drumkit.

Technique can become an issue when dealing with two consecutive eighth notes, either starting on the beat or leading into the beat. Practice the exercise below to get your "doubles" fluid. Play the hi-hat on "2" and "4" when practical. Make sure you play at different tempos. Once mastered, improvise with it!

Track 28

Track 29

Play choruses of different tunes at different tempos utilizing exclusively the "rhythmic unison" approach.

Track 30
(one chorus of "Take the 'A' Train")

By adding anticipations, we not only enhance our cymbal patterns with more variations, we also create a sort of "bump in the road" sensation in the rhythmic flow. If the "bump" is on the "and of 2" or the "and of 4," there's a pushing effect; if it's on the "and of 1" or the "and of 3," the flow pulls back. Anticipations are usually played in rhythmic unison between the ride cymbal and either the snare drum or the bass drum.

Below we have some four-bar phrases utilizing "anticipations." Practice them using the same procedure as you did earlier on page 25.

We can "break it up" even more by adding the "bash" sound to the anticipations. This is done by striking the ride cymbal with the shaft of the stick just under the bead. It will give another sonority as well as add excitement. Jack DeJohnette, Billy Hart, and Bill Stewart use the "bash" sound often and effectively. The "bash" will be notated by an accent over a ride cymbal note.

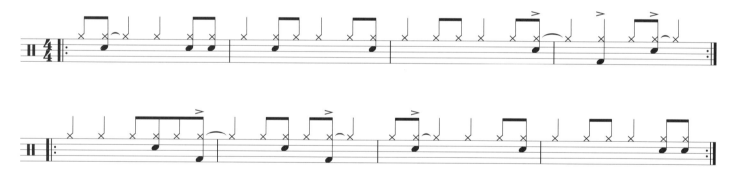

Play choruses on any tune, using exclusively the "rhythmic unison" approach. Include "anticipations" and "bashes" in your improvisation.

Track 31
(one chorus of "Tune Up")

Now let's take a look at the "linear" approach. To start with, try to conceptualize this as one big, varied cymbal rhythm distributed around the drumset. We do this by substituting any of the "ands" normally played on the cymbal, for either the left hand, bass drum, or hi-hat.

To get the idea, first play the following four-bar cymbal rhythm.

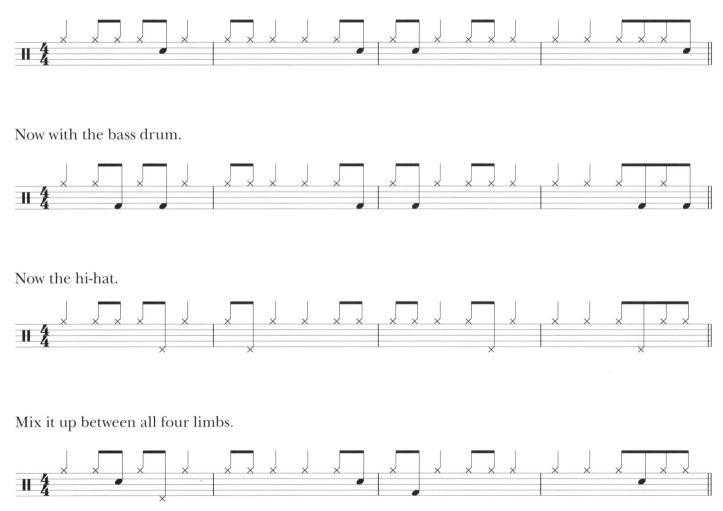

Now, randomly start to substitute some of the "ands" for another part of the drumset, first with the snare drum.

Now with the bass drum.

Now the hi-hat.

Mix it up between all four limbs.

Now improvise a cymbal rhythm over any tune and substitute at will any of the "ands" you would have played on the ride cymbal for another part of the drumset. Try to get the effect of "passing the ball," that is, the listener never knows which sound will be played on the "ands." Try not to be predictable!

Track 32
(one chorus of a blues)

We can also substitute any of the "ands" normally played by the ride cymbal for either of the triplet figures below.

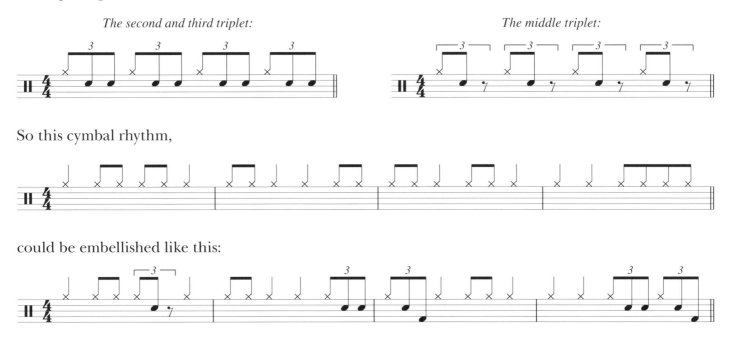

The second and third triplet: *The middle triplet:*

So this cymbal rhythm,

could be embellished like this:

As you can see (and hear), I've substituted some of the "ands" in the cymbal rhythm for one of the triplet figures.

Track 33
(one chorus of a blues)

Play a chorus using exclusively the "linear" approach. Apply the above triplet figures as well as the previously learned eighth-note ones.

Now try adding ruffs and flams to your eighth-note vocabulary!

Play some more choruses, applying some flams and ruffs!

An exception to the linear approach is when you have two consecutive eighth notes where one of them coincides rhythmically with the cymbal and the other doesn't. We call this "half linear" doubles.

Experiment with the different combinations available to you between the left hand, bass drum and snare drum. Practice the exercises below to get together your "half linear" doubles.

 Track 34

Now play several choruses of any tune using exclusively the "linear" approach. Include "half linear" doubles in your improvisation as well as the other learned "linear" techniques.

 Track 36
(one chorus of "Bye Bye Blackbird")

Another form of "half linear" doubles occurs when the second and third part of the triplet is played with any combination of the snare drum, bass drum, or hi-hat and the third part of that triplet rhythmically coincides with the ride cymbal. For example:

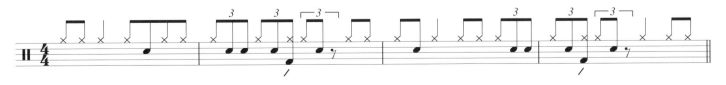

The exercise below is designed to help you to hear and physically feel the difference when the ride cymbal rhythmically coincides with the third part of the triplet and when it doesn't.

Track 37

The same goes for three-note groupings. Develop your ear and your coordination with the exercise below.

Track 38

Add the above triplet figures into your repertoire and play choruses using all of the learned "linear" approach techniques.

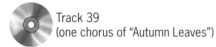

Track 39
(one chorus of "Autumn Leaves")

Now that you've mastered the "rhythmic unison" and "linear" approach separately, it's time to unify them. The best way to do that is to forget about them! You're probably scratching your head right now saying, "What do you mean, forget about them?" Well, keep in mind that these different approaches are designed so that you "hear" everything you play, with no wasted notes and no playing patterns on "automatic pilot." If you've mastered all the exercises, you should be able to do just that! So, just put it all together. Don't think about which approach you're playing; just hear it, and play it! Play many choruses of different tunes at different tempos. Don't worry about tensions, just groove!

TENSIONS RESOLVING ON THE "AND OF 4"

In the '60s, as the cymbal rhythms became more sophisticated, so did the tension devices. One notable aspect was how the tensions didn't always resolve on the "1." Although not always the case, the "and of 4" became the more common.

We can find plenty of figures that resolve on the "and of 4" in our previously learned bebop vocabulary. The resolution note (the "and of 4") can be treated various ways. When played by the left hand, you can either play it:

as written   *as an anticipation*   *or as an anticipation with a "bash" sound.*

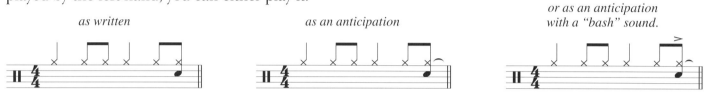

The more subtle choice is when it's played as written. The anticipation gives more emphasis to the resolution, and if it's anticipated with the "bash" sound, even more.

When the resolution (the "and of 4") is played with the bass drum, you have all of the above options, plus you can simultaneously play the left hand on the left side crash or the open hi-hat.

Practice both ways, with the left hand and without.

Here are the rest of the figures, first in eighth notes , then in triplets. Play choruses, including one of the figures at the end of each section of the tune. Use the following patterns as beats "3" and "4" in the last bar of each section of the tune.

Track 40
(one chorus of "There Is No Greater Love")

When resolving on the "and of 4" at the end of a section, there are some very typical figures that are played in the next measure (the first bar of the next section).

These two are quite common.

The following are also used:

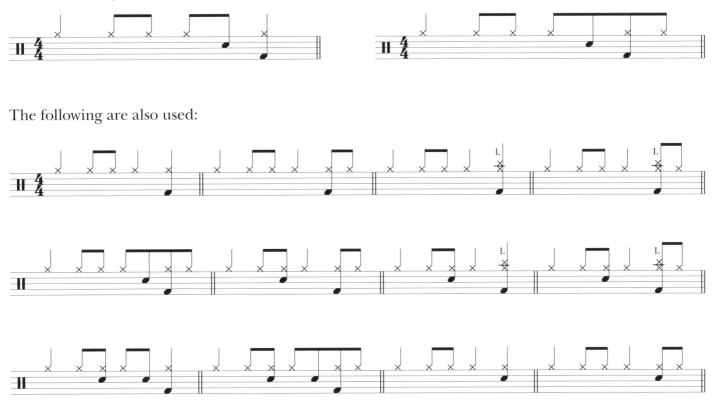

33

Now let's see how to combine the varied cymbal rhythms with their embellishments, the tension figures that lead up to the resolution (the "and of 4") at the end of the section, and the figures played in the first bar of the next section.

For the first seven bars we're playing time, embellishing cymbal variations. In the eighth bar we combine two figures from the bebop vocabulary that resolve on the "and of 4." In the first bar of the new section, we play one of the preceding figures.

Utilizing the above formula, play choruses on any tune that has eight-bar sections.

Resolution Figures with Cymbal Variations

When it comes to tension figures, very often the ride cymbal will adapt to what the rest of the kit is doing, rather than vice-versa. It's more common with eighth-note figures to use the "rhythmic unison" approach. This gives the figure more "muscle," which makes it more dynamic.

In the following pages you'll find one-bar tension figures where the ride cymbal does just that. As with the previous bebop vocabulary, these figures are to be used to lead into a new section of the tune and can be resolved either as written (a more subtle way), as an anticipation, or an anticipation with a "bash" sound. When the resolution note (the "and of 4") falls on the bass drum, you may or may not want to support it with the left hand playing either the left-side crash or open hi-hat. Also, keep in mind that the volume of the figure can make it sound anywhere from subtle to explosive. If you want a more subtle approach, just play the traditional ride pattern on the cymbal with the snare drum and/or bass drum figure sounding underneath.

On those figures that are written on just the cymbal and snare drum lines, feel free to substitute any snare drum hit with the bass drum. On those written figures that include the bass drum, you can substitute hi-hat for the bass drum hits.

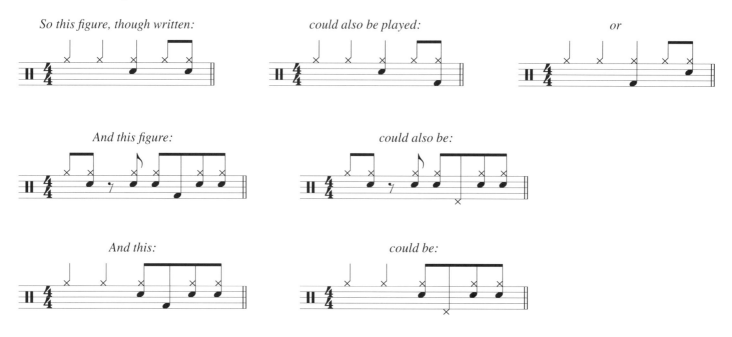

After experimenting with different snare drum, bass drum, and hi-hat combinations on the following figures, play choruses in the following manner: play time with varied cymbal rhythms and their embellishments. In the last bar of the section include one of the figures below, followed by one of the learned figures to be played in the first bar of the new section.

Track 41
(one chorus of "But Not for Me" featuring Figures 4, 8, 12, and 16a)

For the busy figures like 16, I've written out some of the more common bass drum/snare drum combinations.

Track 42
(two choruses of "What Is This Thing Called Love?" featuring Figures 18, 29, 31d, 36, 45, 52, 64, and 69b)

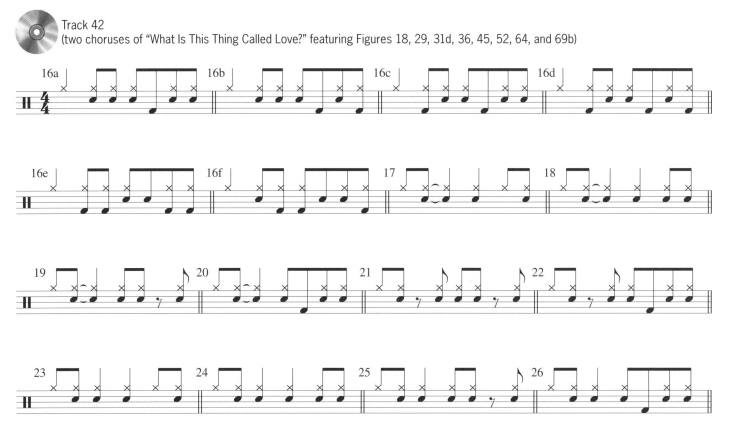

Track 43
(one chorus of "Just Friends" featuring Figures 71, 80, 82b, and 83d)

Two-Bar Tensions

We can create two-bar tensions by simply combining any two of the one-bar tension figures in the previous pages. Here are just some of the many possibilities.

Practice by playing choruses; use these figures in the last two bars of each section. Remember, don't ever count measures, let your singing guide you!

Track 44
(two choruses of "Softy as in a Morning Sunrise")

Time

Triplets, when phrased in note groups of two or four, are great tension devices. Practice the exercises on the next page as written, going from one to the next without stopping. You can also play the accented note on another cymbal. Also substitute hi-hat for any single bass drum note. Although the resolution is written for the "and of 4," you can also resolve on the "1" of the following measure.

Once mastered, play choruses, using these figures as tensions at the end of a section.

Track 46
(one chorus of "Lullaby of Birdland")

40

This page has been left blank to facilitate page turns.

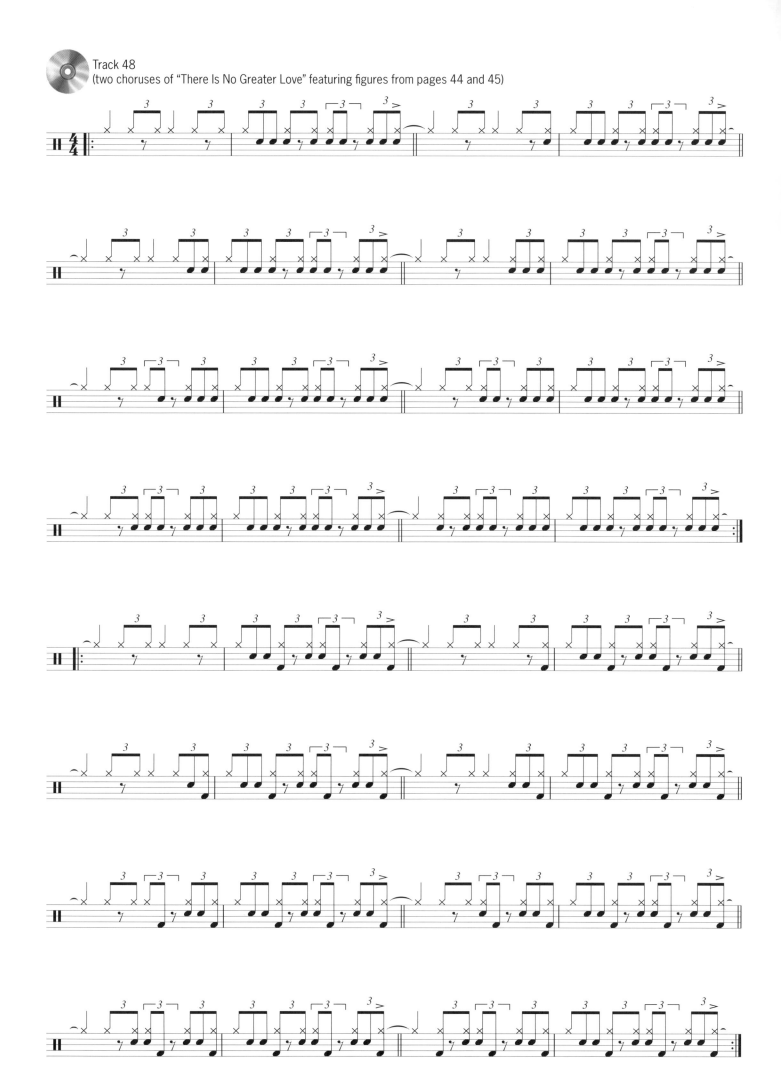

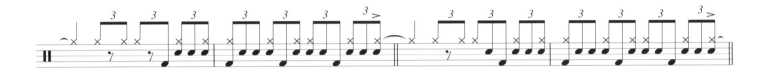

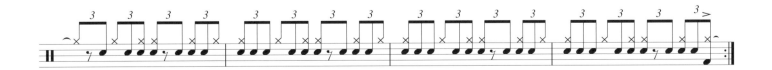

Track 49
(two choruses of a blues featuring figures from page 46)

Track 50
(two choruses of "Bye Bye Blackbird") utilizing the below figures as the last four bars of each section

buzz   buzz   buzz   buzz

ALTERNATIVE RESOLUTION POINTS

Although the "and of 4" and certainly the "1" are common places in the measure to resolve tensions, you can actually resolve them anywhere.

Let's take some examples from the previous one-bar tension figures that resolve on the "and of 4" and see how to resolve them on different parts of the measure.

To resolve on "1," simply carry the figure into the "1" of the next measure (the first bar of the new section).

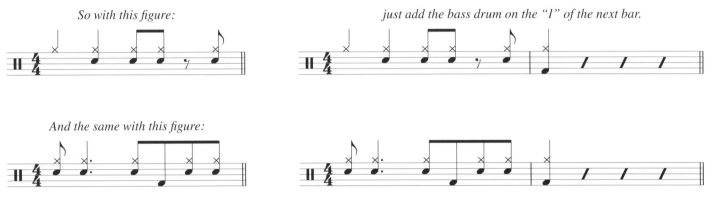

Take any of the one-bar or two-bar tension figures and practice resolving them on "1" instead of the "and of 4".

To resolve on the "4," take any of the tension figures that have a hit on beat "4" and cut off the last note (the "and of 4"). If you want to give the resolution more emphasis, play a bash on the cymbal.

Go back to the figures that resolve on the "and of 4" and and convert them into figures that resolve on "4." Then play choruses on a tune, applying resolutions on "4."

Track 51
(one chorus of "Tune Up")

We can find figures that resolve anywhere in the measure by following the same process.

To resolve on the "and of 3," find a figure that already includes the "and of 3" and simply shave off the last beat.

So this figure: *becomes this:*

Or: *becomes this:*

For a resolution on "3," do the same, only now, keep in mind that you have to fill out the rest of the measure with time on the ride cymbal.

(The ride cymbal fills out the 4th beat.)

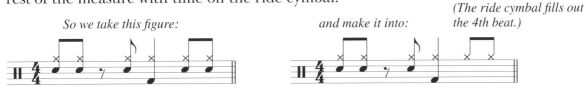

So we take this figure: *and make it into:*

Practice playing resolutions on other parts of the bar by following the same process. As an exercise, play choruses where you always resolve in the same place in the measure. Once that's comfortable, start to vary it.

Track 52
(one chorus of "I Love You" utilizing alternative resolution points)

Another device for alternative resolution points is to play "through the bar," that is, the tension continues into the first measure or measures of the next section before resolving. This gives the sensation of prolongation.

It doesn't resolve until the "2" of the next bar (the first bar of the new section).

Here is the tension figure in the last bar of the section:

Time   **Time**

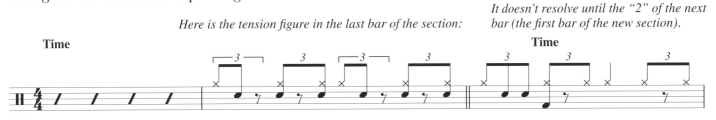

Practice by playing choruses of a tune where you sustain the tensions into the first bar (or bars) of the new section.

Track 53
(one chorus of "How High the Moon")

EXTENDED TENSION TECHNIQUES

The following pages deal with extended tension techniques, that is, ways of creating tension for extended periods of time (more than two bars). These devices, when used tastefully, will help make the music more exciting and hopefully inspire soloists to play at a higher level of intensity. As you practice and learn about these techniques, be sure to hunt for examples in your listening. Consult the "Drummers You Should Check Out" list on page 78; concentrate more on the drummers listed from the '60s to the present, but also listen to how Art Blakey and Max Roach approached extended tensions.

The "extended tension material" that you'll be studying is musically very powerful. Try not to abuse it. It's your secret weapon that you can call up at anytime. You don't want to be like a karate expert that goes out and looks for fights. Be patient, wait for the music to develop, then try to take it to a higher place. See the page on "Pacing" (page 77) for more about this.

Phrasing the Ride Cymbal in Three

One of the most powerful tension devices in jazz is to play what sounds like a 3/4 figure repetitively over the swinging 4/4 structure. This process of playing figures of a different time signature over the one you're actually playing is called superimposing. The trick in doing this, once again, is to use the tune as your guide, not to count measures. As a start, though, you may want to see how it mathematically works out. We're going to start with just the ride cymbal.

Let's see how this cymbal pattern in 3/4 lays over 4/4 time.

As you can see, it takes three measures to complete itself.

If you were to extend it, here's how it would lay over a 12-bar blues structure. It goes on for an entire chorus before it resolves itself within the structure.

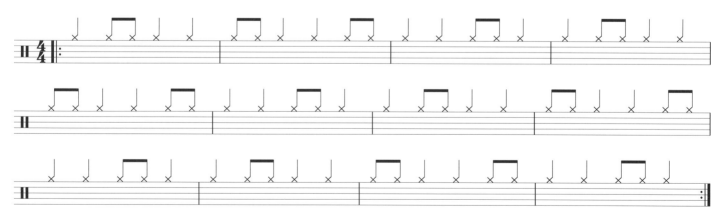

Track 54
(singing two choruses of the blues while superimposing 3/4 over the 4/4 structure)

Now practice playing the previous cymbal pattern (play just the cymbal) while singing a blues. Be able to do it without looking at the page. This is the key! Once you can do that, play varied cymbal patterns over the blues; be able to inject the repeated 3/4 cymbal pattern anywhere in the structure. You need to have the ability to stop and start it wherever you hear it. Don't count measures; let the tune guide you.

Now let's take the same figure and put it in an eight-bar structure. In this case, the figure takes 24 bars before it resolves itself within the eight-bar structure. In order to play the figure through an entire 32-bar chorus, play through the entire 24-bar cycle, then add on the first eight bars.

Do the same with a 32-bar standard as you did with the blues.

Track 55
(superimposing 3/4 over 4/4 while singing "Jingle Bells")

Embellishing the Ride Cymbal Phrased in Three

Now that you've seen and heard how the superimposed 3/4 cymbal works over a 4/4 song structure, let's see how we can dress it up.

Although in the first 32 figures, the cymbal is accompanied by a snare drum line only, feel free to substitute any snare drum hit with the bass drum or any other part of the drumset. For the rest of the figures, sometimes substitute the hi-hat for the bass drum. Also try using flams and ruffs on the snare drum notes that don't correspond rhythmically with the cymbal as well as the left hand on the left side crash or open hi-hat with single bass drum hits.

Be able to play any one of these figures repetitively over an entire chorus of any song structure. This way you'll be able to stop and start them anywhere you want. Also play choruses and use these figures as tensions to be resolved wherever you see fit.

Track 56
(one chorus of "Take the 'A' Train" featuring figures 5, 10, 14, and 20)

The following "anticipation" figures are very effective. Freely substitute snare drum notes with the bass drum or any other part of the kit. In the figures where there are bass drum notes written, replace some of them with hi-hat.

Track 58
(one chorus of "But Not for Me" featuring figures 61, 65, 69, and 74)

Here are some triplet figures for your vocabulary.

Track 59
(one chorus of "Autumn Leaves" featuring figures 85, 97, 103, and 109)

Track 60
(one chorus of "Bye Bye Blackbird" featuring figures 152, 168, 176, and 183)

Track 61
(one chorus of "There Is No Greater Love" featuring figures 275, 278, 286, and 294)

Snare Drum Lead

The ride cymbal is not always the main voice in a jazz drummer's accompaniment. Sometimes it will shift to another part of the drumkit. This sudden color change makes for a nice tension device. In this part of the study, the snare drum will be the lead voice, a technique we will refer to as "snare drum lead."

When playing "snare drum lead," first think of the rhythm you want to play with the left hand on the snare drum. The right hand follows the left hand by playing rhythmic unison (the same rhythm on the ride cymbal), while the bass drum fills in the holes (the missing eighth notes).

Step 1. Play something like cymbal variations, but on the snare drum.

Track 62

Step 2. Now add the cymbal in rhythmic unison.

Track 63

Finally: fill all the missing eighth notes with the bass drum:

Track 64

Or the hi-hat:

Track 65

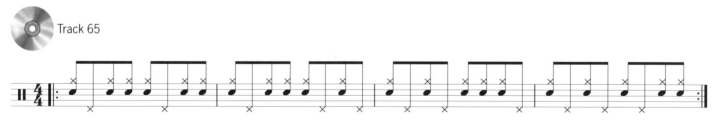

Or any combination of the two:

Track 66

Play choruses on any tune, employing the "snare drum lead" technique as a tension device in the last two, three, or four bars of the different sections of the tune.

Track 67
(one chorus of "Tune Up")

Here are a few more figures you can use. Remember always to hear the snare drum as the "lead" voice.

Play several choruses of any tune, applying any of the above figures as a tension figure.

Track 68
(one chorus of "Softly as in a Morning Sunrise")

"Snare drum lead" figures also work as great tension devices when using the superimposed 3/4 technique.

*Feel free to substitute the hi-hat for any single bass drum hit.

Be able to play any of the above 3/4 figures repetitively for an entire chorus of any tune. Then play choruses using any one of these figures as tension devices.

Track 69
(one chorus of "I Got Rhythm")

Bass Drum Lead

Playing the bass drum as the lead voice also makes for a very exciting tension device. In this case, the bass drum has the principal voice, which is backed up by the same rhythm on the cymbal with a "bash" sound while the left hand fills in the missing eighth notes.

Concentrate on the rhythm you want to play on the bass drum rather than the general rhythm, which is a steady stream of eighth notes.

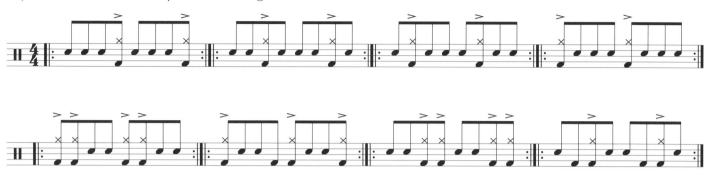

Here are some "bass drum lead" figures in 3/4. Be able to play them repetitively for an entire chorus.

Try playing "bass drum lead" with the following 12-bar figure over a blues.

 Track 70

Now try playing an entire blues chorus using your own rhythms and applying the "bass drum lead" technique.

Track 71
(one chorus of "Softly as in a Morning Sunrise")

Here are some sparse bass drum rhythms that call for some specific stickings. The first is a paradiddle-diddle, the second and third a double paradiddle.

As always, be able to play these patterns repetitively over an entire chorus of any standard in 4/4 time, then try to play some choruses applying the above figures as well as any other "bass drum lead" figures as tension devices.

Track 72
(one chorus of "Just Friends")

Snare Drum and Bass Drum Lead

If we combine the techniques of snare drum lead with bass drum lead, we have even more possibilities.

Once the tempo starts to get brighter, you might want to leave some of the cymbal notes out.

The four-bar phrase below starts with a snare drum lead figure in three. Note that the accents indicate when it's bass drum lead.

With figures like the previous ones, the trick is to simplify it as you see it in the example below. Hear the main line, fill in the missing notes, and let the cymbal follow.

Below we have a 16-bar example that combines snare drum lead with bass drum lead made up of just the important notes. Below that we have the same example completely written out with the "filler" notes and the cymbal included. Try to play it only looking at the top example, using the bottom as a reference for any doubts you may have. Try also substituting the hi-hat for the bass drum.

Track 73

With Filler Notes

Practice your own four-bar combinations, then eight bars. Play choruses, using similar figures as tension devices.

Track 74
(one chorus of "I Love You")

Bass Drum Lead in Triplets

Bass drum lead in triplets, a technique without a doubt invented by Elvin Jones (although I doubt he had a name for it), in concept is the same as bass drum lead in eighth notes in that you play a syncopated figure with the bass drum and adorn it with the rest of the kit. However, the triplet element makes this technique a bit more sophisticated.

The idea is to have a constant stream of triplets, while the bass drum outlines the syncopated eighth-note rhythm that you hear in your head. To achieve this constant barrage of triplets, we start with the following figure:

Track 75

So if your bass drum rhythm is this:

Any bass drum hits on the beat fit in quite naturely:

Track 76

However, if your bass drum rhythm includes hits on the "ands," like this:

Then replace the snare drum notes that coincide with the rhythmic line for bass drum notes. This will, of course, always fall on the third part of the triplet.

Track 77

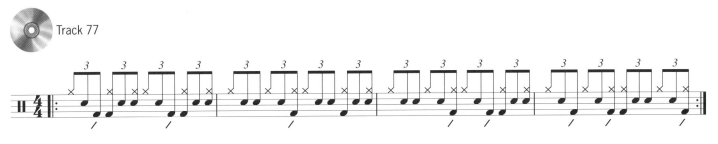

If we want to combine "cymbal variations" with bass drum lead in triplets, we use the same basic approaches that we used earlier when embellishing the cymbal variations, that is, "rhythmic unison" and "linear."

The "rhythmic unison" approach is the following:

1. When there's no activity in the bass drum or a bass drum hit on the beat, here's your basic pattern: quarter notes on the cymbal, with the second and third triplet played by the left hand. (In the example below, there's a bass drum hit on the 4th beat.)

2. Whenever you play the bass drum on an "and," play the cymbal with it.

3. The same goes for doubles starting on an "and."

4. The same goes when starting on the beat (the first and third part of the triplet).

Play the following 16-bar rhythm as the lead voice for "Bass Drum Lead in Triplets" using the "rhythmic unison" approach. If you get stuck, the whole thing is written out on the next page.

Track 78

With Filler Notes

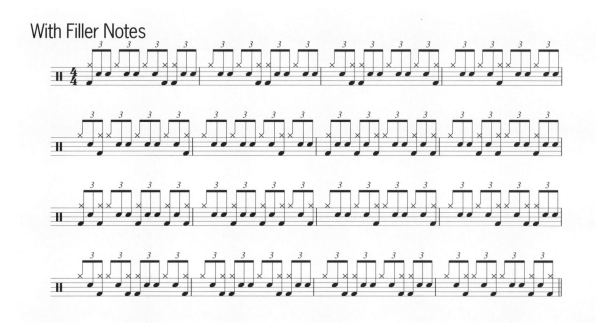

Try playing entire choruses using this technique, then also play choruses using it as a tension device.

To play "Bass Drum Lead in Triplets" using the "linear" approach, we start by being able to play any cymbal variation over the following left-hand pattern:

For example:

Track 79

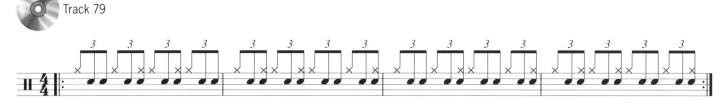

As strictly an exercise, practice playing choruses using cymbal variations over the left-hand figure.

Step 2 is to substitute any of the "ands" in your cymbal rhythm with your bass drum, like for example:

Track 80

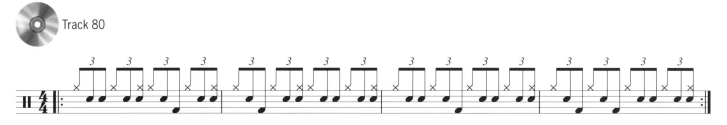

Practice the two following patterns:

Now try playing choruses, substituting any "and" you would have played on the cymbal with the bass drum.

 Track 81
(one chorus of a blues)

Once you're comfortable playing choruses with the above, step 3 is to add some single bass drum hits on the beat (that will, of course, hit at the same time as the ride cymbal), maybe something like this:

Now try playing choruses, substituting any "and" you would have played on the cymbal with the bass drum, as well as bass drum hits on the beat.

 Track 82
(one chorus of a blues)

Step 4 is to include double hits on the bass drum, starting on the "and," such as:

Practice these two basic patterns:

Now play more choruses, this time including double bass drum hits that start on an "and."

 Track 83
(one chorus of a blues)

Step 5 is to include bass drum hits that fall on the first and third part of the triplet, which in eighth-note language would be a double starting on the beat. Such as:

Practice these two basic patterns:

Now play more choruses, this time including doubles that start on the beat.

Track 84
(one chorus of a blues)

The last step for mastering triplet bass drum lead using the linear approach is to conceive it directly from the rhythmic line that you are going to play with your bass drum. To do this, create the bass drum line, then fill in the other parts of the drumset as practiced earlier.

So if our rhythmic line for the bass drum is:

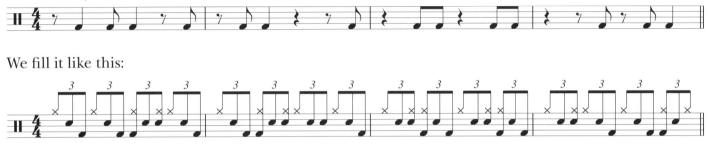

We fill it like this:

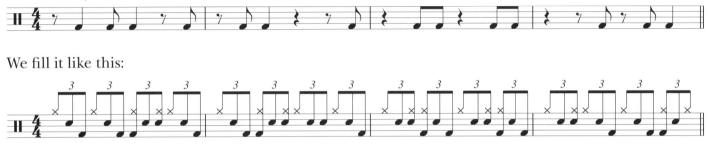

Try embellishing the following bass drum line using the "linear" approach to "Bass Drum Lead in Triplets." On the bottom of the page you have it written out entirely.

Track 85

With Filler Notes

Once the previous example is mastered, play choruses on your own improvised bass drum rhythm.

Track 86
(one chorus of a blues)

Now let's see how we can combine the "rhythmic unison" and "linear" approaches to "Bass Drum Lead in Triplets." The main difference is the treatment of bass drum hits that fall on the "ands." With the "unison" approach it hits with the cymbal, and with the "linear" it doesn't. All bass drum hits that fall on the beat will hit with the ride cymbal with either approach.

In the examples below, we can combine the two different approaches with the same 3/4 bass drum figure.

Unison Approach: **Linear Approach:**

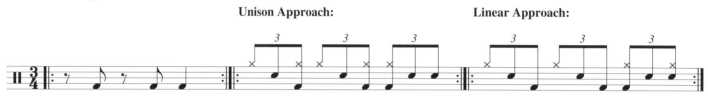

You can combine the two approaches different ways, depending on how you hear it.

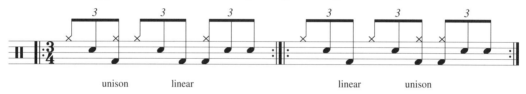

Play through the following exercises to develop the skill of combining the two approaches. Before each exercise, you have the bass drum line written alone.

1.

2.

Embellish the below 32-bar written bass drum line combining, as you wish, the two approaches ("rhythmic unison" and "linear") to playing "Bass Drum Lead in Triplets."

Track 87

Create your own rhythmic line and embellish it, combining the two approaches while singing any tune. Also play choruses using these techniques as tension devices.

Track 88
(one chorus of "Take the 'A' Train")

Another way to play "Bass Drum Lead in Triplets" is to approach it the same way we did with eighth notes, that is, play the cymbal (with a "bash" sound) with the bass drum, filling in the missing triplets with the left hand.

So,   would be:

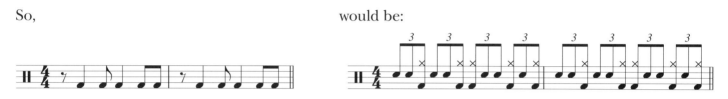

Notes of a dotted-quarter value or more can present a sticking problem if you can't or don't want to play all the fill-in notes with the left hand.

The suggested sticking for the line is:

As you can see for the dotted-quarter note, we're using the following sticking.

With half notes, a paradiddle-diddle sticking works well.

Play the following line using the bass drum lead technique described on the the previous page. In this exercise, the fill-in notes are all played by the left hand. If you have any doubts, consult the bottom of the page.

Track 89

With Filler Notes

Now play an entire chorus of any tune applying this technique. Once you can do that, bring the technique into context by using it as a tension device.

Track 90
(one chorus of "Lullaby of Birdland")

In medium to slow tempos, combinations that include the middle triplet or those phrased in groups of two or four notes are quite dynamic sounding.

Once comfortable with the above figures, play choruses, using any one or any combination of them to create tension at the end of a section. Resolve them on the "1" of the new section.

Track 91
(one chorus of "Autumn Leaves")

Bombs Away

One way that many jazz drummers create a lot of tension is to momentarily play on top of the band (volume wise) with a series of accents, thus creating a momentary chaotic effect that begs for release. This tension device, sometimes referred to as "dropping bombs," can be very exciting when used tastefully, but be careful; this powerful tool can be very annoying when in the wrong hands.

These explosive bursts often come out in two-note combinations.

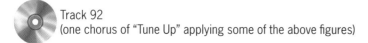

Track 92
(one chorus of "Tune Up" applying some of the above figures)

3/4 figures are very effective.

As a start, practice using this technique as a tension device at the end of a section in a tune. Then, practice "dropping bombs" anywhere in the structure. This device is particularly effective in trumpet solos à la Miles Davis, Woody Shaw, and Freddie Hubbard, where the soloist asks a musical question and then waits for an answer.

 Track 93
(one chorus of "Just Friends")

Here are four ways of creating extended tensions using the "explosion" effect, all based on the same idea. Art Blakey was a master of these types of tensions.

3.

R L R L R R L R   L R L L L R L R L   R R L R L R L L   R L R L R R L R

L R L L R L R L   R R L R L R L L   R L R L R R L R   L R L L R

Time

4.

Time

Track 94
(two choruses of "I Got Rhythm" with each of the written figures leading into the bridge and the top)

A more subtle way of achieving this effect, particularly for piano solos or any other low-volume setting, is with cross-sticks (the kind you use for bossa novas), as in the below (also à la Art Blakey) figures.

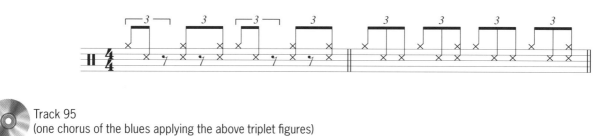

Track 95
(one chorus of the blues applying the above triplet figures)

Be able to play an entire chorus with the following three-bar phrase. This way you'll be able to start or end it anywhere in the structure that you hear it.

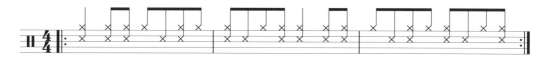

Here's the same idea, but with the cymbal in 3/4. Practice it the same way as you did with the previous figure.

Track 96
(one chorus of the blues applying some of the above 3/4 figures)

PACING

Track 97
(three choruses of "What Is This Thing Called Love?")

Usually, soloists like their solos to build. In other words, the solo ends at a higher intensity than when it starts out. The time that it takes to get from the lower intensity to the higher is called "pacing." In order to calculate your pacing as an accompanist, it's helpful to have a general idea of how long the solo will be. If it's only going to be one chorus, the intensity has to rise quickly, as opposed to three or four choruses where the band can take its time and build gradually. Although you may not know the exact length of the solo (unless it's talked about ahead of time) by listening and musically knowing the soloist, you should have a pretty good idea.

As the drummer, you have three basic parameters to work with to control the intensity: the degree of the tension (which is dictated by how much you disrupt the even 4/4 flow), the length of the tension, and the volume at which it's played. Keep in mind that the instrumentation will dictate your dynamic (volume) range. For example, a piano solo would have a smaller range than, say, a trumpet solo. In fact, in your listening, you should have noticed that it's quite common for drummers to go to a lighter sounding ride cymbal for the piano solo.

To develop the concept of pacing, try playing a set amount of choruses of a tune, first two, then three, four, even up to five choruses. Try to make each chorus more intense than the one before, almost as if you're shifting into a higher gear each chorus. In the first chorus, start with a minimum of volume; just groove with the ride cymbal and then build it from there. Don't give too much too soon, and when you get to the last chorus, try to give the impression that you could always give a little more if you needed to.

Also, practice the same exercise, but take away the volume parameter. That is, play various choruses at a low volume, maintain that volume, but still build the intensity from chorus to chorus with your tensions.

And last, don't miss the opportunity to practice this concept with other musicians. They have to work on building from chorus to chorus also; it's not all on your shoulders.

Drummers You Should Check Out!

It's essential that you listen to the great jazz drummers from the past to the present. Here is a list to get you started, somewhat in chronological order:

Kenny Clarke, Max Roach, Art Blakey, and **Philly Joe Jones** were very influential from the bebop period up through the '50s. Other important drummers from this period include: **Alan Dawson, Jimmy Cobb, Frankie Dunlop, Billy Higgins, Lawrence Marable, Ben Riley, Art Taylor, Ed Thigpen, Denzil Best, Lex Humphries, Frank Gant, Ed Blackwell, Frank Butler, Connie Kay, Stan Levy, Mel Lewis, Shelly Manne, Larry Bunker, Vernel Fournier, Charles Moffett, Charli Persip, Al Harewood, Donald Bailey,** and **Micky Roker,** among others.

When the '60s came around, the innovative stylings of **Elvin Jones** and **Tony Williams** changed jazz drumming forever. Their innovations, particularly how the ride cymbal was approached, created a sort of "new school" in drumming. Certain great drummers, already established in the '50s, like **Roy Haynes, Dannie Richmond, Albert "Tootie" Heath,** and **Louis Hayes** not only made the transition, but did it in their own personal, creative way.

Drummers like **Joe Chambers, Billy Hart, Pete LaRoca Sims, Jack DeJohnette,** and **Grady Tate** also made their mark in the '60s.

The end of the '60s into the '70s brought wonderful drummers like **Idris Muhammad, Al Foster, Eddie Gladden, Victor Lewis, Peter Erskine, Alex Riel, John Dentz, Freddie Waits, Michael Carvin, Joe LaBarbara,** and **Jimmy Madison.** The end of the '70s was also a springboard for the careers of dynamic drummers like **Kenny Washington** and **Adam Nussbaum.**

Tony Reedus, Marvin "Smitty" Smith, Terri Lyne Carrington, Lewis Nash, Ralph Peterson, Billy Drummond, Carl Allen, Byron Landham, and **Jeff "Tain" Watts** came into prominence in the '80s and are drummers you should definitely listen to.

Also, don't miss drummers like **Brian Blade, Joe Farnsworth, Ari Hoenig, Greg Hutchinson, Cindy Blackman, Clarence Penn, Willy Jones III, Karriem Riggens, Herlin Riley, John Riley, Steve Smith, Bill Stewart, Rodney Green, Joe Strasser, Pete Zimmer, Peter Van Nostrand, Donald Edwards,** and **Mark Taylor.**

This is not by any means meant to be a definitive list; there are many more outstanding drummers out there waiting to be checked out. Keep your eyes and ears open!

Listening Guide

Listening to the music is just as important as practicing and playing. It gives you the chance to hear how different masters of this art form handle different situations. I have found, however, that students seem to be confused on what they should be listening for. It's not just about waiting for that really cool drum lick and trying to figure it out (though that certainly is a part of it).

In this section, we will see how to listen and what to listen for, and relate it directly to the practiced studies learned in the previous pages of this book.

- Let's assume we're talking about a straight-ahead jazz tune, since that's the subject matter of our study.

- Before you start to listen to a track, know the **name of the tune**.

- The first time through, don't bother listening attentively to the drummer. Instead, concentrate on the composition and what the other instruments are doing.

- Composition wise, try and learn **the melody** and definitely investigate **the form**. Is it a **blues**? **AABA**? **ABAB**? **An alternative structure**?

- What is **the bass** doing? Does he play the melody **"in 2"** (half notes)? or is he **walking** from the get-go? Are there any **pedals** or **ostinatos**? Is there a **Latin vamp** in the structure?

- How does the **piano player comp**? Does he leave a lot of **space** or is his comping more **dense**? Does he stop playing at times in the horn solo? Where does he **resolve** the end of the sections? Is it **sometimes/usually/always/never on "1"** or the **"and of 4"**?

- Does the **solo build**? Is the soloist **more intense at the end** of the solo than at the beginning?

Once you've established the above, start zooming in on the drummer.

- How is he playing the ride cymbal? Is it with a strong **quarter-note pulse** or is it with a **three-note motion starting on beats "2" and "4"**?

- Is the **ride cymbal varied** or is it pretty much the **traditional ride rhythm**?

- Try to hear **how** each left-hand hit on the **snare drum relates to the ride cymbal**. That is, does the hit **coincide with the cymbal** or does it fall **in between cymbal notes**?

- When (or if) **two consecutive eighth notes** are played with any combination of either the left hand, bass drum, or hi-hat (doubles), are they **"unison"** or **"half linear" doubles**?

- After **each section** of the tune, did the drummer create any **tension**, or is he just **comping**?

- When the drummer does create a tension, **where** does he **resolve** it? Is it **on the "1"**? The **"and of 4"**? Does it **coincide** with what the **piano player** played? Or does he **resolve it earlier** in the measure? Or does he play **through the "1"**?

- Is the **tension** a **triplet figure** or more eighth-note based?

- Is the figure the **same or similar** to any of the **figures** that you've studied? If so, **which ones?**

- Do you **recognize** any of the tension techniques studied such as **snare drum** or **bass drum lead** figures?

- Are there **more frequent and longer tensions** as the **solo builds?** **How so?**

Now, let's say the drummer plays something you really like and you want to "borrow it." As you're lifting it, apart from the obvious, **what** is the figure? Make sure you also know:

Where are you in the **structure?** Also, **where in the measure** does the figure fall?

How is he playing it? Is it **loud, soft?** What is the **balance** within the drumset? Is the **cymbal predominant? The snare? The bass drum?** (Be careful, recordings can be deceiving as far as balance is concerned.) Which are the **accented notes?**

When is he playing the figure? Is it in the **beginning, middle,** or **end of the solo?** Is it at a **climatic part of the solo?**

As you can see, you should play a track many times in order to listen for all the points mentioned above. I hope that you find these suggestions useful, as they should make your listening sessions more productive and your practicing more meaningful.

Epilogue

If you've studied the system in this book, done the required listening, mastered all of the exercises, and put all the techniques and concepts into practice, you will have made an incredible amount of progress in your ability to play in a straight-ahead jazz situation. However, there is one last important step that may be the most important of them all. It was, perhaps, best expressed to me by the great alto saxophonist Lee Konitz.

I was working with Lee and bassist Santi DeBriano in trio at the Café Central in Madrid. Before the first set, Lee called Santi and me over and said he wanted to talk to us. He said, "I was thinking, we could play a tune, and each one of us could be playing in a different time signature! I could play in 4/4, Santi, you play in 3/4, while Jeff plays in 5/4, you know, *polymeter*!" Santi and I nodded politely and Lee continued, "In fact, we don't even have to be playing the same tempo! I could be playing a medium tempo, Santi a ballad tempo, and Jeff could be at a cooking, fast tempo, you know *polytempo*!" Santi and I nodded again, shrugged our shoulders, looked at each other as if to say, "Who are we to argue with Lee Konitz" and went up to the bandstand to start the first set. Lee called "Body and Soul"; he and Santi would play the first chorus in duo. They started to play and the time started to stretch and stretch, and stretch some more, until they were at two different parts of the tune. Santi wisely stopped playing and left Lee on his own. Lee continued playing by himself for a few bars, then suddenly stopped playing, took the horn out of his mouth, turned to the audience, and yelled "*polymeter, polytempo, Polly want a cracker?*" This was Lee's humorous way of saying, "Okay, that's enough intellectual nonsense, let's just play," and that's precisely what we did.

The last step in learning any system, technique, or concept that has to do with the arts is to forget about it! If you've really worked at it, then it's a part of you; let it go. If you're able to do that, then you just might sometimes get to that place where all musicians want to be, which is where you no longer play the instrument, it plays you!

About the Author

Jeff Jerolamon began playing drums when he was nine years old. He took lessons in Red Bank, N.J. with teachers Dave Brewer and Art Magyar. He received his early jazz education from high school band director Ken Walters, drum instructor Tony DeNicola at Trenton State College, and Stu Martin at The Creative Music Studio in Woodstock, N.Y. He also studied music composition with William Humenay. He moved to New York in 1976 where he worked as a freelance musician until moving to Valencia, Spain in 1982. Over his career Jeff has performed with such jazz greats as Junior Cook, Joe Henderson, Lee Konitz, Lou Donaldson, Tal Farlow, Wallace Roney, George Cables, and John Hicks, among others. He also subbed a week with the Count Basie Orchestra under the direction of Frank Foster and has done drum shows with legends such as Louie Bellson and Arthur Taylor. Currently, apart from a busy performing schedule, Jeff is a faculty member of the jazz department at the Valencia Conservatory (Conservatorio Superior de Musica de Valencia) and teaches privately at APB Drums (Asociacion de Baterías y Percusionistas De Valencia).